If Dinosaurs were Cats ̄

Colin McNaughton

MATHEW PRICE LIMITED

ISBN 1-84248-128-2 hardback
ISBN 1-84248-129-0 paperback

Imagine giant snakes and hogs,
 King-size parrots, jumbo frogs.
If dinosaurs were cats and dogs
 Just think of the trouble there'd be . . .

Mince is on the Menu

Pigplodicus, immensely fat,
  The countryside his habitat,
He chases butchers' vans till, splat!
  Mince is on the menu.

Watch him go, he's streaky bacon.
  Butchers terrified and shaken.
Inevitably overtaken –
  Mince is on the menu!

Bombs Away!

The farmworkers are praying
    'Cause the chickasaurs are laying
And there's no way of delaying
    When the chickasaurs let fly.

Country life is not romantic
    With a hen coop that's gigantic
And the farmworkers are frantic
    When the chickasaurs let fly.

Don't Tangle with a Kangasaur

Don't tangle with a Kangasaur
    Just hop it, find the nearest door
You'd end up knocked out on the floor –
    He's champion of the world.

But if you must, then jink and jive,
    Bob and weave and duck and dive.
It's your only chance to stay alive –
    He's champion of the world!

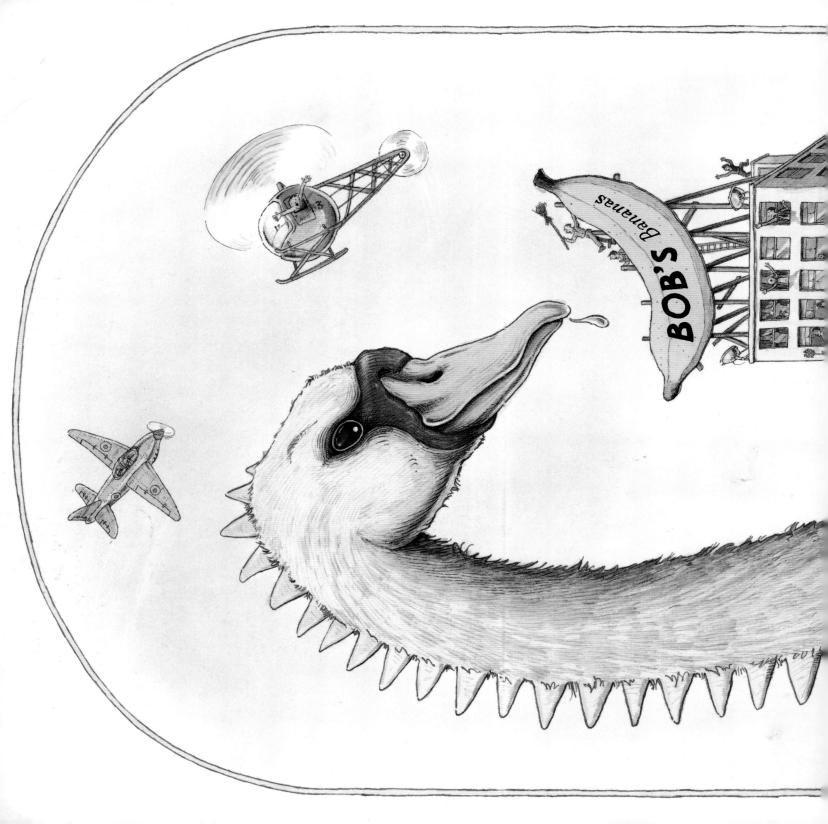

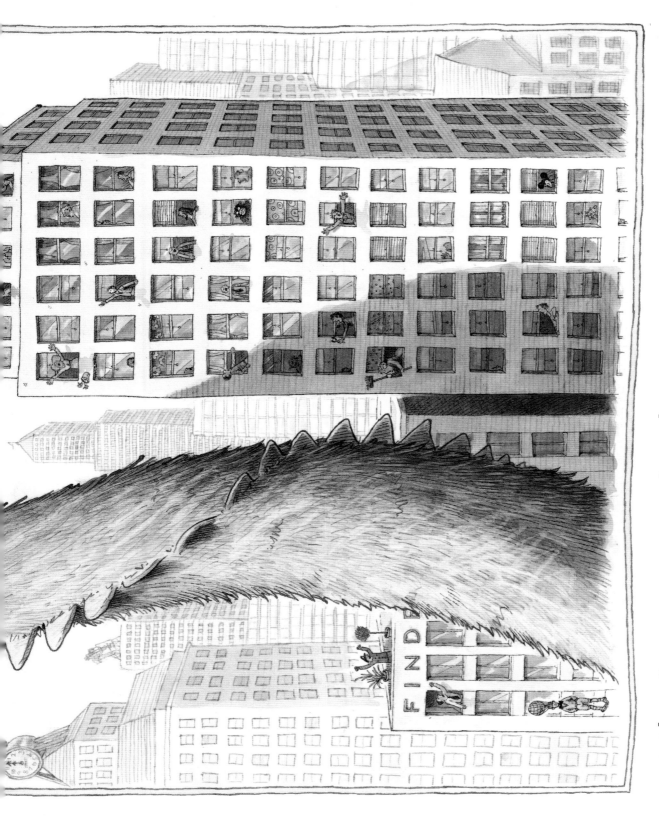

The Swantosaur's Flaw

O graceful soaring swantosaur,
  You just go up, and then some more.
I must admit you have one flaw:
  Your favourite food is human!

Ripe bananas, fresh or fried,
  There's a thousand things you haven't tried.
So how on earth can you decide
  Your favourite food is human?

The Snakeydon

The long and the short of the Snakeydon
Is that he just goes on and on

And on and on and on and on

And on and on and on and on

And on and on and on and on

And on and on and on and on

And on and on and on and on

Do not Disturb

Oh, do not wake the Tortosaur.
The terrible, mountainous Tortosaur.
The Tortosaur's a carnivore –
He'll have your guts for garters.

The Fabulous Parrodactyl

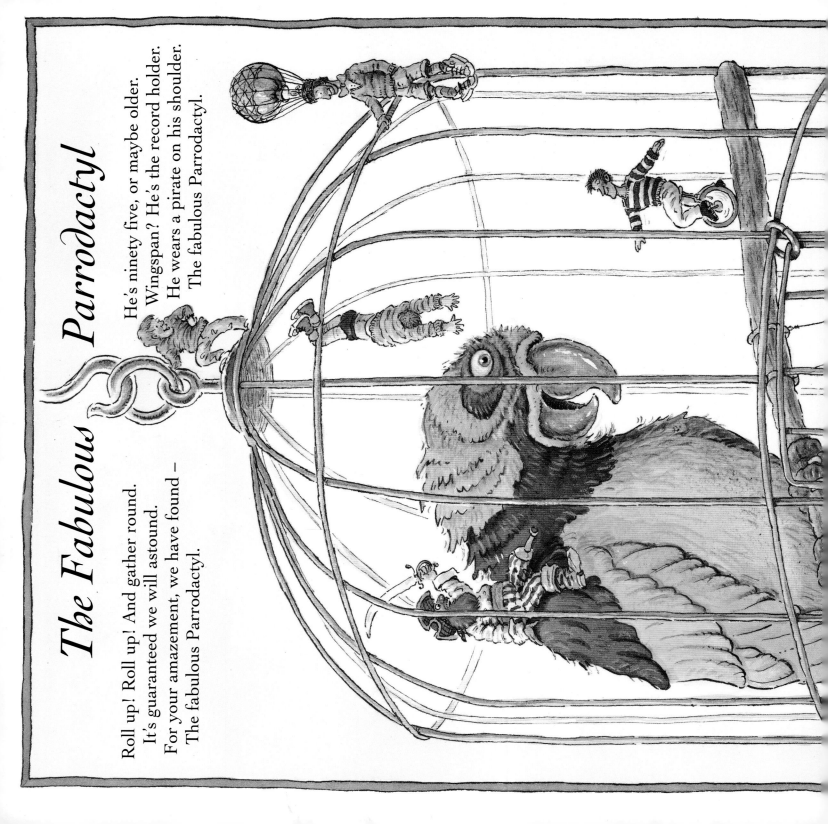

Roll up! Roll up! And gather round.
It's guaranteed we will astound.
For your amazement, we have found –
The fabulous Parrodactyl.

He's ninety five, or maybe older.
Wingspan? He's the record holder.
He wears a pirate on his shoulder.
The fabulous Parrodactyl.

The Moleosaurus

My lawn will never be the same,
   The cricket's ruined, crying shame.
The moleosaurus, he's to blame.
   There ought to be a law.

My gardener's a mountaineer.
   Now we've got mountain goats, not deer.
O, Moleosaurus – disappear!
   There ought to be a law.

The Frogosaurus

They fly through the air
　　With the greatest of ease
The daring young man
　　On a frog, if you please.
Their movements are graceful,
　　They float on the breeze,
Tally-ho! Action Stations!
　　Hoorah!

Hedgeyhogeyplodicus

Hedgeyhogeyplodicus,
   I really hate to make a fuss
But must you always pick on us,
   It's getting rather boring.

So there you have it – flying frogs,
King-size parrots, giant hogs.
If dinosaurs were cats and dogs,
Just think of the trouble there'd be.